Liberty Phi

# ARIES

# INTRODUCTION

Astrology is all about the planets in our skies and what energy and characteristics influence us. From ancient times, people have wanted to understand the rhythms of life and looked to the skies and their celestial bodies for inspiration, and the ancient constellations are there in the 12 zodiac signs we recognise from astrology. The Ancient Greeks devised narratives related to myths and legends about their celestial ancestors, to which they referred to make decisions and choices. Roman mythology did the same and over the years these ancient wisdoms became refined into today's modern astrology.

The configuration of the planets in the sky at the time and place of our birth is unique to each and every one of us, and what this means and how it plays out throughout our lives is both fascinating and informative. Just knowing which planet rules your sun sign is the beginning of an exploratory journey that can provide you with a useful tool for life.

Understanding the meaning, energetic nature and power of each planet, where this sits in your birth chart and what this might mean is all important information and linked to your date, place and time of birth, relevant *only* to you. Completely individual, the way in which you can work with the power of the planets comes from understanding their qualities and how this might influence the position in which they sit in your chart.

What knowledge of astrology can give you is the tools for working out how a planetary pattern might influence you, because of its relationship to your particular planetary configuration and circumstances. Each sun sign has a set of characteristics linked to its ruling planet – for example, Aries is ruled by Mars – and, in turn, to each of the 12 Houses (see page 81) that form the structure of every individual's birth chart (see page 78). Once you know the meanings of these and how these relate to different areas of your life, you can begin to work out what might be relevant to you when, for example, you read in a magazine horoscope that there's a Full Moon in Capricorn or that Jupiter is transiting Mars.

Each of the 12 astrological or zodiac sun signs is ruled by a planet (see page 52) and looking at a planet's characteristics will give you an indication of the influences brought to bear on each sign. It's useful to have a general understanding of these influences, because your birth chart includes many of them, in different house or planetary configurations, which gives you information about how uniquely *you* you are. Also included in this book are the minor planets (see page 102), also relevant to the information your chart provides.

# ARIES

O ur sun sign is determined by the date of our birth wherever
we are born, and if you are an Aries you were born between
March 21st and April 19th. Bear in mind, however, that
if you were born on one or other of those actual dates it's worth
checking your *time* of birth, if you know it, against the year you
were born and where. That's because no one is born 'on the cusp'
(see page 78) and because there will be a moment on those days
when Pisces shifts to Aries, and Aries shifts to Taurus. It's well worth
a check, especially if you've never felt quite convinced that the
characteristics of your designated sun sign match your own.

The constellation of Aries, named from the Latin word for the
ram, is one of the medium-sized ones in our skies. Its arrangement
of three stars includes the brightest one Hamal (Alpha Arietis), the
name of which is derived from the Arabic meaning 'child of a sheep'.
In Greek mythology, a ram was sent to save the life of the young
prince Phrixus, and in gratitude its life was sacrificed to Zeus, king of

the gods, and its golden fleece treasured, going on to feature in the story of Jason and the Argonauts.

Aries is ruled by the planet Mars, the Roman god of war, and who the month March is named after. There's much to be said for Mars' strongly positive energy, which can be harnessed and put to good use, giving Aries the gift of courage and passion.

A fire sign (like Leo and Sagittarius), Aries has the ability to literally fire up others with their enthusiasm and get things started, leading from the front and encouraging others by inspiring them through courageous ideas and acts. Aries is a cardinal sign (like Cancer, Libra and Capricorn) and all about action, excited by competition and thrives on the chase, preferring to get things done immediately rather than ponder over the consequences of their actions. And therein lies a small note of caution, as Aries can sometimes head off into the fray before they've really thought things through. But they are capable of learning through experience and not making the same mistake twice.

The sign ♈ of Aries shows the horns and long skull of the ram, and indicates the direct nature of this sign's character, happy to dive head-first into a situation and initiate action.

## PHYSICAL POWER
Aries rules the head, and many born under this sign might find they are troubled by headaches and migraines, occasional bumps to the head or minor injuries to the face.

## SACRED GEMSTONE
Diamond, produced naturally under conditions of high temperature and pressure and symbolic of how Aries performs under pressure. Once faceted and cut, these precious gems literally sparkle with an inner fire. Clear quartz applies too.

## OPPOSITE SIGN
Libra

Depicted by the ram, unafraid to push ahead if necessary to gain pole position, Aries' me-first attitude can often be seen as rather selfish but, in reality, they are often the cheerleaders and instigators of change for others. The first sign of the zodiac, associated with new beginnings and the beginning of each year's cycle, there's something open and optimistic and almost child-like about their enthusiasm for life. And while some Aries may resort to tantrums or sulks to get their own way, this behaviour seldom lasts long.

For Aries, life is an adventure and one they approach with anticipation that it will work out well, an attitude that helps them navigate the rough and the smooth, the twists and turns, with optimism even when the going gets tough. But there's a tendency to focus on the journey rather than the destination; the excitement

Aries feels may rest more in anticipation of an event rather than its actual occurrence. Because of this constant looking towards the next big thing, Aries sometimes loses out on the pleasure and satisfaction of actually completing something and one life lesson can be in learning to appreciate the here and now, rather than always looking towards what comes next.

That's one of the downsides to being ruled by Mars: its dynamism can bring a restlessness. It can sometimes be difficult to balance being constantly on the move with the staying power to get things completed. Some Aries have a list of unfinished tasks because they become bored before completion, and they have to learn the satisfaction of focusing their energy on getting things *done* as well as getting things *started*.

Aries is also intensely loyal and once a commitment is made to another, it takes a lot to break it. That said, if someone lets them down they may be quick to anger but then they usually forgive and forget. Aries seldom holds a grudge but moves swiftly on to the next project or person, excited once again by a new beginning. All of which can get rather exhausting for those that Aries lives or works with and the ram needs to take this into account when trying to chivvy the rest of the flock into action.

So while it's worth Aries making the most of their Mars energy, its independent spirit, courage and ability to inspire others, there are always accommodations that can be usefully made to help ensure others have the opportunity to recognise the generosity, intuitiveness and warm-hearted love they also offer. Temper that energetic fire with a little humility, pausing to give time to just *be* rather than endlessly doing, and also allow others to nurture you. Aries need to make themselves available to accept love and attention, otherwise it's hard for others to feel properly connected to their Aries friend, lover or family member.

# THE MOON IN
# YOUR CHART

While your zodiac sign is your sun sign, making you a sun sign Aries, the Moon also plays a role in your birth chart and if you know the time and place of your birth, along with your birth date, you can get your birth chart done (see page 78). From this you can discover in which zodiac sign your Moon is positioned in your chart.

The Moon reflects the characteristics of who you are at the time of your birth, your innate personality, how you express yourself and how you are seen by others. This is in contrast to our sun sign which indicates the more dominant characteristics we reveal as we travel through life. The Moon also represents the feminine in our natal chart (the Sun the masculine) and the sign in which our Moon falls can indicate how we express the feminine side of our personality. Looking at the two signs together in our charts immediately creates a balance.

# MOON IN ARIES

The Moon spends roughly 2.5 days in each zodiac sign as it moves through all 12 signs during its monthly cycle. This means that the Moon is regularly in Aries, and it can be useful to know when this occurs and in particular when we have a New Moon or a Full Moon in Aries because these are especially good times for you to focus your energy and intentions.

A New Moon is always the start of a new cycle, an opportunity to set new intentions for the coming month, and when this is in your own sign, Aries, you can benefit from this additional energy and support. The Full Moon is an opportunity to reflect on the culmination of your earlier intentions.

## NEW MOON
### IN ARIES AFFIRMATION

'I am at one with the energy of fire and feel its power
to lift my heart and soul, pay heed to its power and
trust its ancient strength to cleanse and
support me.'

## FULL MOON
### IN ARIES AFFIRMATION

'I am born of fire and I will use this symbolic
energy to revitalise and revive, and to move more
purposefully in my life's direction.'

# ARIES HEALTH

Aries rules the head, so headaches and migraines can be an occasional or recurring problem, along with head injuries. But in addition to this it's important to remember that all that high-octane activity for which Aries is known can also create a downside, the sort of physical and mental exhaustion that can lead to mental health problems.

In fact, the downside of this Mars energy is that Aries may push on further and harder than they can physically manage, and burnout can easily be a side effect of this. Learning to pace themselves is a life lesson useful for Aries to learn sooner rather than later. Relentless endeavour can give way to fatigue, anxiety and depression, because even courageous Aries isn't completely immune to the pressures of life. Allowing head space for rest and relaxation may not come easy and may take time to learn, but the wise Aries will realise their stamina is well served by regular time out.

Naturally Aries is drawn to competitive exercise, but factoring in some regular activities that allow for physical and mental downtime – running or yoga might fit the bill here – can recharge those batteries and avoid burnout.

# POWER UP
# YOUR ARIES
# ENERGY

There are often moments or periods when we feel uninspired, demotivated and low in energy. At these times it's worth working with your innate sun sign energy to power up again, and paying attention to what Aries relishes and needs can help support both physical and mental health.

Reconnect with the fire in your sign by getting out into the sunlight. Whatever the season, the Sun's rays will reinvigorate. Whether it's the gentle winter sun or the summer's beneficial heat (wear sunscreen!), you can be sure that its energy will give Aries a lift. Even just the natural daylight will help lift your mood, especially if your work life relies on artificial light. It's particularly important when the weather has put a dampener on Aries' natural *joie de vivre*, so even a brisk walk between showers will help raise energy levels and the spirits, and all the better if it's through natural surroundings where Aries can also gain inspiration from the changing seasons.

Aries can also recharge their batteries by spending time with other people, as that independent spirit may find them spending long hours working alone or caught up in their own heads. It may be that communal activities which have a contemplative edge – watercolour painting, perhaps? – will help reconnect the thinking mind to the feeling heart while pressing pause on physical activity. Balancing Aries' restless energy with a gentle focus on art or the natural world goes a long way in helping them wind down. Sleep can sometimes prove elusive when they are wound up, so finding ways to soothe and calm that active brain and allow for peaceful, restorative sleep is an important aspect of how Aries can restore their energy and zest for life.

Nurturing the physical body is important too. Aries can be haphazard eaters and although they seldom overeat, they may eat less than nutritiously. To sustain Aries, it's important to consider nutrition and choose those foods that can either fire them up or, if overstimulated, calm the physical body and support the mind. Look to grains and root vegetables to ground and earth energy, along with decaffeinated drinks like chamomile teas. And when Aries needs to lighten things up and rekindle that fire, look to foods with a bitter edge: dark leafy greens like kale and spinach, yoghurts and lemon-based dishes. Add a touch of cayenne pepper, garlic and ginger to stimulate the appetite by making foods tasty but avoid too much salt.

Utilise a New Moon in Aries with a ritual to set your intentions and power up: light a candle, use essential oil of vetiver to lift your mood and concentration (this oil blends well with calming rose and stabilising bergamot), focus your thoughts on the change you wish to see and allow time to meditate on this. Place your gemstone (see page 13) in the moonlight. Write down your intentions and keep in a safe place. Meditate on the New Moon in Aries affirmation (see page 21).

At a Full Moon in Aries you will have the benefit of the Sun's reflected light to help illuminate what is working for you and what you can let go, because the Full Moon brings clarity. Focus on this with another ritual, taking the time to meditate on the Full Moon in Aries affirmation (see page 21). Light a candle, place your gemstone in the moonlight and make a note of your thoughts and feelings, strengthened by the Moon in your sign.

# ARIES'
# SPIRITUAL
# HOME

K nowing where to go to replenish your soul and recharge your batteries both physically and spiritually is important and worth serious consideration. For some Aries, contemplating the flames of an open fire on safari may be their spiritual home and many may also earn their living through travel and adventure, while others may find their direction in some way that stimulates their inventiveness and creativity.

Wherever they hail from, there are also a number of countries where Aries will feel comfortable, whether they choose to go there to live, work or just take a holiday. Countries that are dynamic like Germany, Poland, England and Zimbabwe have similar astrological properties to Aries and feel comfortable to them.

When it comes to holidays, activity holidays have an immediate attraction, so many Aries will recharge their batteries by using physical energy to ski, surf, trek or kayak, while others look to replenish their fire through less energetic means, visiting cultural hotspots like Florence, Manhattan or Berlin. But wherever they holiday or take a break, Aries needs to be reinvigorated in mind as well as body.

# A R I E S

# W O M A N

There's usually something immediately recognisable about an Aries woman, the directness of her gaze, the energy of her movements, the spontaneity of her freedom-loving soul. This is a woman who is never idling in the shallows, but always on the lookout for the next big thing. Her mental energy is reflected in her physical energy with a tendency towards brisk and efficient movements and a trim physique.

Her open manner attracts others and she usually has a diverse range of friends and likes nothing more than to organise a fun event to bring people together to socialise. A generous host, she may have a tendency to over organise, wanting to take care of everything, so learning to allow others to help her is a useful lesson, otherwise it's all too easy to take on too much and burn out. This is when stress headaches can become a problem and some downtime is needed.

But Aries is the most loyal of friends and, once her heart is given, the most committed of lovers. She may wear her heart on her sleeve, which is characteristic of her straightforward approach to life, but she doesn't in fact give her heart up completely so easily.

There's a touch of caution before she'll give away something so precious, but when she does she's in it's 100 per cent. An Aries woman isn't always easy to love either. That independent streak can come across as too bossy and domineering for some, but is often a cover and masks a deep need for love and a long-term relationship. She will still need to be won over, however, even if she's convinced by 'the one' because, as the saying goes, *faint heart never won fair woman*. It takes a certain sort of maturity in a partner to recognise her sterling qualities and love her just as she is because what you see is what you get, which can be wonderful.

No one loves quite as ferociously as an Aries woman, either. This is a woman who will move heaven and earth for those she loves, particularly as a mother, but who can also be quite beguilingly tender-hearted, capable of the most gentle of thoughtful gestures; her intuition is another of her qualities. Don't underestimate her ability to tune into you and genuinely understand where someone's head and heart is. Truly she is a diamond and one to be cherished.

# ARIES

MAN

This big-hearted man doesn't hide his feelings under a bushel and can be direct to a fault. Do you like this new hairstyle, you may ask? The answer will be an unequivocal yes or no, as they are nothing if not forthright. Old-fashioned courtesies may not be too evident but he will accord you the same independence of opinion as for himself, and respect any straightforward response if he's missing the point. What he can't really manage is game-playing, passive aggression or too much subtlety, as he tends to be quite literal in his understanding and call a spade a spade, expecting you to do likewise. Because, really, life's about getting on with it and he'd rather not waste time trying to second guess what it is you want or mean: just tell him.

That said, all the energy and spontaneity and youthful optimism that marks out the first sign of the zodiac makes Aries a very attractive man, seldom short of admirers. That youthfulness often extends to their looks, and even when they are grey-haired there's a spring in their step,

sparkle in their eye and an enviably trim waistline that immediately knocks off the years. It's not vanity that means they keep their looks, they haven't got time to preen, but good basic self-care and an inclination towards an energetic lifestyle that comes naturally to Aries.

In a social group, Aries often stands out because he's the one making sure everyone else is having a good time, even if he's not the actual host. He will often seek out the underdog and help them gain confidence and shine because his big heart doesn't want anyone left out. It may be hard to get his undivided attention but once you do, it's yours and if the stars align could be yours for life. However, he's also a man that loves a challenge and the thrill of the chase so although he doesn't play games himself, a would-be lover may have to use this Aries knowledge to their advantage and not be *too* easily available, playing hard to get and demonstrating the sort of independence, imagination and energy Aries recognises and is attracted by.

# ARIES IN
# LOVE

Ruled by warrior-like Mars, Aries can approach love much like a knight on a quest, enjoying the challenge and the chase. One of the things they are looking for is assurance that they are number one in anyone's life; taking second place doesn't come naturally to Aries, being the first sign of the zodiac.

It's not all about the physical either, for Aries. Their active mind and imagination will seek out someone with similar mental energy and although intrigue isn't part of their repertoire, they are easily intrigued by someone who enjoys discussing art, politics, music, philosophy and even sport, with an original viewpoint. This is not a sign that follows the herd but one whose views tend to be ahead of the curve, with an interest in the new rather than the old. A first bond can be intellectual for Aries, before it moves on to a deeper, erotic commitment.

# ARIES AS
# A LOVER

Unsurprisingly being ruled by Mars, energy – and imagination – lies at the heart of Aries' lovemaking; they can be surprisingly intuitive and sensual, so don't underestimate them or write them off as perfunctory lovers. The mind is a powerful aphrodisiac and this isn't wasted on Aries, for whom foreplay is important, not an *hors d'oeuvre*, and this may start long before the bedroom. As a fire sign, even when they are slow to kindle, once that spark has been ignited it's hard to put out.

When it comes to making love, Aries isn't averse to more adventurous aspects of sex, and while role playing and bondage might feature, they will always prefer to be the one in charge. In addition, a deep affection for their lover will always temper their eroticism because, at that moment, Aries is always in love with their lover and seeking the *grande amore*, which is very much their life's goal.

Aries tends to wear their heart on their sleeve, and once committed give it completely, they are generally unafraid to say how they feel and what they want, and expect the same in return. For the more cautious, this can sometimes feel overwhelming, and in these cases Aries might need to review their tactics. For them, the challenge and the chase is also part of the action and very much part of the fun too, but they need to recognise it's not always the same for others.

Loyalty is important and any jealousy on the part of Aries seldom comes from lack of security but from the sense that they are not *numero uno* in their lover's eyes. They have to come first; it takes a more mature Aries to learn that someone may not *always* prioritise them, but as long as they normally do, that's not the end of the world.

Υ

# WHICH SIGN
# SUITS ARIES?

I n relationships with Aries, the sun sign of the other person and
the ruling planet of that sign can bring out the best, or sometimes
the worst, in a lover. Knowing what might spark, smoulder or
suffocate love is worth closer investigation, but always remember
that sun sign astrology is only a starting point for any relationship.

## ARIES
## AND ARIES

Mars and Mars together could make the sparks fly although they do have a unique understanding of what each other needs, a combination of commitment and freedom that ensures their needs are met.

## ARIES AND
## TAURUS

Mars and Venus are already lovers in mythology, and fiery Aries is gently earthed, bringing stability to the relationship, while firing up and inspiring Taurus' more placid nature. There's definitely devotion and loyalty.

## ARIES AND
## GEMINI

Gemini's wilfulness and mind games can alternatively bewitch and bewilder Aries, their mercurial influence and airy nature kindling the sparks of a relationship, but there's a tendency to flare too bright and burn out in the end.

## ARIES AND CANCER

Mars is captivated by the Moon's mysterious light and Cancer's need for security will often put Aries in the number one spot – which can work brilliantly, as long as they both acknowledge a need for freedom and avoid dampening the fire.

## ARIES AND LEO

Two outrageous fire signs with Leo ruled by the Sun, the most egotistical fire of all, might be too much even for freedom-loving Mars but often their physical relationship is so great that the tussle for who is king (or queen) pin doesn't matter.

## ARIES AND VIRGO

Virgo's earthiness is ruled by Mercury, ensuring there is a capacity to intrigue Aries' Mars without being too heavy handed and restricting that freedom-loving fire, lightening the impact of any criticism of the fire sign's more impulsive actions.

## ARIES AND
## LIBRA

Venus rules Libra, bringing an airy
balance to this relationship with
Mars. It may have been written
into mythology but it still requires
attention if Aries is to recognise
this for the potentially harmonious
connection it can be.

## ARIES AND
## SCORPIO

At first glance, Pluto's regenerative
energy may not look so attractive
to Mars and while Scorpio's hidden
depths take time to discover, Aries
is often well rewarded by a return
in commitment that is more than
superficial as both like to bond for life.

## ARIES AND
## SAGITTARIUS

Freedom-loving Jupiter can make a
happy connection to equally freedom-
loving Mars, as long as they both
recognise that fidelity is also necessary
for a relationship between these two
sun signs to flourish, because Aries
can't tolerate disloyalty.

## ARIES AND CAPRICORN

Saturn's self-discipline can be good for Mars' youthful exuberance and as long as Capricorn exercises a light touch, Aries often responds happily to the sort of boundaries that also represent security and loving commitment.

## ARIES AND AQUARIUS

Both Uranus and Mars have freedom-loving aspects but Aquarius' commitment to humanity might irk the fire sign's need to be number one in their lives, and Aries may need reassurance and encouragement to commit to campaigning together.

## ARIES AND PISCES

Neptune's sensitivity and imagination means Pisces easily responds to that aspect of Aries, if not their need for independence that can undermine the water sign's need to be needed and put a dampener on the relationship.

# ARIES AT WORK

Work of some sort is essential to an Aries' ego and they often feel defined by what they do almost as much as who they are and this is why you often see them in leadership or public-facing roles. For the majority of Aries, this is a comfortable place to be as they are seldom backstage. Even when part of a team, their confidence often finds them leading it just by being energetic, imaginative and enthusiastic even if they have to learn from their elders once in a while.

Although Aries is often financially successful, money is not a particular incentive to work, rather it is the graft itself that excites them, especially if it's a project they have conceived themselves, even if that's within a larger corporation. What is important to Aries though is that they are recognised by their peers for their efforts and are adequately acknowledged for their part in the success of a project. Often though, Aries' entrepreneurial streak finds them happiest running their own show or working in a freelance capacity.

They are prepared to take risks too and because of a combination of their intuitive and competitive streak, these are often successful.

That risk-taking can also find Aries in high-octane activities: firefighters, the military, financial traders, actors and journalists and other occupations where an adrenaline surge is grist to their mill. But that leadership can also necessitate a quieter, more sustained energy, and teaching, some form of social work or politics (local or national) that also require good decision-making might also suit Aries. Few Aries stay at entry level for long, but they may also choose to branch out alone, or head up a competitive business rather than hang around waiting for promotion.

It may take Aries a while to find a career that suits them best, so allowing some early exploration into different fields is never a wasted experience and often helps focus early ideas into something more enduring and rewarding. With such youthful energy and enthusiasm, making a few twists and turns in the early years will actually yield interesting opportunities and those experiences are invaluable if they are learnt from.

# ARIES AT HOME

Home is important to Aries partly because it creates an essential hearth for their fire, but also because it's somewhere secure to return to after fighting the good fight and overcoming life's challenges. Home is part fortress, part sustenance. Generous to a fault, the sentiment *mi casa es tu casa* doesn't always apply, and some may guard their privacy fiercely. However, once an invitation is extended, it's completely open and any visitor is made welcome, but family tends to always come first. That's probably as it should be and family is often why Aries creates a home in the first place, security for their partner and children, or their pets: peel back that fighting spirit and you find that family is what it's all about when it comes to settling down.

The kitchen is a space for entertaining in an energetic and informal way. No grand dinner parties – spontaneous kitchen suppers are more Aries' style. Large, tasty casseroles, baked potatoes, huge pasta dishes and mixed salads, thrown together from great ingredients, that provide sustenance and happy socialising after a hard day's work are par for the course. Aries tends to be fairly well organised when it comes to their creature comforts and counts food as one of life's necessities rather than a luxury.

The bricks and mortar of Aries' home are less important than the comfort they seek from it and there are often beautiful soft furnishings in warm colours and sumptuous fabrics in warming tones and from far-flung places. Terracotta walls, dupion silks, Moroccan kilims, original paintings, wooden artefacts collected from various travels, all give colour and texture to Aries' surroundings. Inevitably, the biggest room in the home will also have a fireplace of some sort, and a view. Being able to see beyond the immediate horizon gives Aries a sense of freedom even when they're enjoying the accommodation and security of home.

# FREE THE
# SPIRIT

U nderstanding your own sun sign astrology is only part of
the picture. It provides you with a template to examine and
reflect on your own life's journey but also the context for
this through your relationships with others, intimate or otherwise,
and within the culture and environment in which you live.

Throughout time, the Sun and planets of our universe have
kept to their paths and astrologers have used this ancient wisdom
to understand the pattern of the universe. In this way, astrology is
a tool to utilise these wisdoms, a way of helping make sense of the
energies we experience as the planets shift in our skies.

'A physician without a knowledge of astrology has no right to
call himself a physician,' said Hippocrates, the Greek physician born
in 460 BC, who understood better than anyone how these psychic
energies worked. As did Carl Jung, the 20th-century philosopher and
psychoanalyst, because he said, 'Astrology represents the summation
of all the psychological knowledge of antiquity.'

THE 10 PLANETS

# SUN

RULES THE ASTROLOGICAL SIGN OF LEO

Although the Sun is officially a star, for the purpose of astrology it's considered a planet. It is also the centre of our universe and gives us both light and energy; our lives are dependent on it and it embodies our creative life force. As a life giver, the Sun is considered a masculine entity, the patriarch and ruler of the skies. Our sun sign is where we start our astrological journey whichever sign it falls in, and as long as we know which day of which month we were born, we have this primary knowledge.

# MOON

We now know that the Moon is actually a natural satellite of the Earth (the third planet from the sun) rather than a planet but is considered such for the purposes of astrology. It's dependent on the Sun for its reflected light, and it is only through their celestial relationship that we can see it. In this way, the Moon in each of our birth charts depicts the feminine energy to balance the masculine sun's life force, the ying to its yang. It is not an impotent or subservient presence, particularly when you consider how it gives the world's oceans their tides, the relentless energy of the ebb and flow powering up the seas. The Moon's energy also helps illuminate our unconscious desires, helping to bring these to the service of our self-knowledge.

# MERCURY

Mercury, messenger of the gods, has always been associated with speed and agility, whether in body or mind. Because of this, Mercury is considered to be the planet of quick wit and anything requiring verbal dexterity and the application of intelligence. Those with Mercury prominent in their chart love exchanging and debating ideas and telling stories (often with a tendency to embellish the truth of a situation), making them prominent in professions where these qualities are valuable.

Astronomically, Mercury is the closest planet to the sun and moves around a lot in our skies. What's also relevant is that several times a year Mercury appears to be retrograde (see page 99) which has the effect of slowing down or disrupting its influence.

# VENUS

The goddess of beauty, love and pleasure. Venus is
the second planet from the sun and benefits from
this proximity, having received its positive vibes.
Depending on which astrological sign Venus falls in
your chart will influence how you relate to art and
culture and the opposite sex. The characteristics of
this sign will tell you all you need to know about
what you aspire to, where you seek and how you
experience pleasure, along with the types of lover you
attract. Again, partly depending on where it's placed,
Venus can sometimes increase self-indulgence which
can be a less positive aspect of a hedonistic life.

# MARS

RULES THE ASTROLOGICAL SIGN OF ARIES

This big, powerful planet is fourth from the sun and exerts an energetic force, powering up the characteristics of the astrological sign in which it falls in your chart. This will tell you how you assert yourself, whether your anger flares or smoulders, what might stir your passion and how you express your sexual desires. Mars will show you what works best for you to turn ideas into action, the sort of energy you might need to see something through and how your independent spirit can be most effectively engaged.

ARIES

# JUPITER

Big, bountiful Jupiter is the largest planet in our solar system and fifth from the sun. It heralds optimism, generosity and general benevolence. Whichever sign Jupiter falls in in your chart is where you will find the characteristics for your particular experience of luck, happiness and good fortune. Jupiter will show you which areas to focus on to gain the most and best from your life. Wherever Jupiter appears in your chart it will bring a positive influence and when it's prominent in our skies we all benefit.

# SATURN

RULES THE ASTROLOGICAL SIGN OF CAPRICORN

Saturn is considered akin to Old Father Time, with all the patience, realism and wisdom that archetype evokes. Sometimes called the taskmaster of the skies, its influence is all about how we handle responsibility and it requires that we graft and apply ourselves in order to learn life's lessons. The sixth planet from the sun, Saturn's 'return' (see page 100) to its place in an individual's birth chart occurs approximately every 28 years. How self-disciplined you are about overcoming opposition or adversity will be influenced by the characteristics of the sign in which this powerful planet falls in your chart.

# URANUS

The seventh planet from the sun, Uranus is the planet of unpredictability, change and surprise, and whether you love or loathe the impact of Uranus will depend in part on which astrological sign it influences in your chart. How you respond to its influence is entirely up to the characteristics of the sign it occupies in your chart. Whether you see the change it heralds as a gift or a curse is up to you, but because it takes seven years to travel through a sign, its presence in a sign can influence a generation.

# NEPTUNE

Neptune ruled the sea, and this planet is all about deep waters of mystery, imagination and secrets. It's also representative of our spiritual side so the characteristics of whichever astrological sign it occupies in your chart will influence how this plays out in your life. Neptune is the eighth planet from the sun and its influence can be subtle and mysterious. The astrological sign in which it falls in your chart will indicate how you realise your vision, dream and goals. The only precaution is if it falls in an equally watery sign, creating a potential difficulty in distinguishing between fantasy and reality.

# PLUTO

Pluto is the furthest planet from the sun and exerts a regenerative energy that transforms but often requires destruction to erase what's come before in order to begin again. Its energy often lies dormant and then erupts, so the astrological sign in which it falls will have a bearing on how this might play out in your chart. Transformation can be very positive but also very painful. When Pluto's influence is strong, change occurs and how you react or respond to this will be very individual. Don't fear it, but reflect on how to use its energy to your benefit.

  ♈ ARIES

# YOUR SUN SIGN

Your sun or zodiac sign is the one in which you were born, determined by the date of your birth. Your sun sign is ruled by a specific planet. For example, Aries is ruled by Mars but Gemini by Mercury, so we already have the first piece of information and the first piece of our individual jigsaw puzzle.

The next piece of the jigsaw is understanding that the energy of a particular planet in your birth chart (see page 78) plays out via the characteristics of the astrological sign in which it's positioned, and this is hugely valuable in understanding some of the patterns of your life. You may have your Sun in Aries, and a good insight into the characteristics of this sign, but what if you have Neptune in Leo? Or Venus in Aries? Uranus in Virgo? Understanding the impact of these influences can help you reflect on the way you react or respond and the choices you can make, helping to ensure more positive outcomes.

If, for example, with Uranus in Taurus you are resistant to change, remind yourself that change is inevitable and can be positive, allowing you to work with it rather than against its influence. If you have Neptune in Virgo, it will bring a more spiritual element to this practical earth sign, while Mercury in Aquarius will enhance the predictive element of your analysis and judgement. The scope and range and useful aspect of having this knowledge is just the beginning of how you can utilise astrology to live your best life.

# PLANETS IN TRANSIT

In addition, the planets do not stay still. They are said to transit (move) through the course of an astrological year. Those closest to us, like Mercury, transit quite regularly (every 88 days), while those further away, like Pluto, take much longer, in this case 248 years to come full circle. So the effects of each planet can vary depending on their position and this is why we hear astrologers talk about someone's Saturn return (see page 100), Mercury retrograde (see page 99) or about Capricorn (or other sun sign) 'weather'. This is indicative of an influence that can be anticipated and worked with and is both universal and personal. The shifting positions of the planets bring an influence to bear on each of us, linked to the position of our own planetary influences and how these have a bearing on each other. If you understand the nature of these planetary influences you can begin to work with, rather than against, them and this information can be very much to your benefit. First, though, you need to take a look at the component parts of astrology, the pieces of your personal jigsaw, then you'll have the information you need to make sense of how your sun sign might be affected during the changing patterns of the planets.

# YOUR BIRTH CHART

With the date, time and place of birth, you can easily find out where your (or anyone else's) planets are positioned from an online astrological chart programme (see page 110). This will give you an exact sun sign position, which you probably already know, but it can also be useful if you think you were born 'on the cusp' because it will give you an *exact* indication of what sign you were born in. In addition, this natal chart will tell you your Ascendant sign, which sign your Moon is in, along with the other planets specific to your personal and completely individual chart and the Houses (see page 81) in which the astrological signs are positioned.

A birth chart is divided into 12 sections, representing each of the 12 Houses (see pages 82–85) with your Ascendant or Rising sign always positioned in the 1st House, and the other 11 Houses running counter-clockwise from one to 12.

# ASCENDANT OR RISING SIGN

Your Ascendant is a first, important part of the complexity of an individual birth chart. While your sun sign gives you an indication of the personality you will inhabit through the course of your life, it is your Ascendant or Rising sign – which is the sign rising at the break of dawn on the Eastern horizon at the time and on the date of your birth – that often gives a truer indication of how you will project your personality and consequently how the world sees you. So even though you were born a sun sign Aries, whatever sign your Ascendant is in, for example Cancer, will be read through the characteristics of this astrological sign.

Your Ascendant is always in your 1st House, which is the House of the Self (see page 82) and the other houses always follow the same consecutive astrological order. So if, for example, your Ascendant is Leo, then your second house is in Virgo, your third house in Libra, and so on. Each house has its own characteristics but how these will play out in your individual chart will be influenced by the sign positioned in it.

Opposite your Ascendant is your Descendant sign, positioned in the 7th House (see page 84) and this shows what you look for in a partnership, your complementary 'other half' as it were. There's always something intriguing about what the Descendant can help us to understand, and it's worth knowing yours and being on the lookout for it when considering a long-term marital or business partnership.

# THE
# 12
# HOUSES

While each of the 12 Houses represent different aspects of our lives, they are also ruled by one of the 12 astrological signs, giving each house its specific characteristics. When we discover, for example, that we have Capricorn in the 12th House, this might suggest a pragmatic or practical approach to spirituality. Or, if you had Gemini in your 6th House, this might suggest a rather airy approach to organisation.

# 1ST HOUSE

### RULED BY ARIES

The first impression you give walking into a room, how you like to be seen, your sense of self and the energy with which you approach life.

# 2ND HOUSE

### RULED BY TAURUS

What you value, including what you own that provides your material security; your self-value and work ethic, how you earn your income.

# 3RD HOUSE

### RULED BY GEMINI

How you communicate through words, deeds and gestures; also how you learn and function in a group, including within your own family.

# 4 TH HOUSE

### RULED BY CANCER

This is about your home, your security
and how you take care of yourself and
your family; and also about those family
traditions you hold dear.

# 5 TH HOUSE

### RULED BY LEO

Creativity in all its forms, including fun
and eroticism, intimate relationships and
procreation, self-expression
and positive fulfilment.

# 6 TH HOUSE

### RULED BY VIRGO

How you organise your daily routine, your
health, your business affairs, and how you
are of service to others, from those
in your family to the workplace.

# 7 TH HOUSE

### RULED BY LIBRA

This is about partnerships and shared
goals, whether marital or in business,
and what we look for in these to
complement ourselves.

# 8 TH HOUSE

### RULED BY SCORPIO

Regeneration, through death and rebirth,
and also our legacy and how this might be
realised through sex, procreation
and progeny.

# 9 TH HOUSE

### RULED BY SAGITTARIUS

Our world view, cultures outside our
own and the bigger picture beyond our
immediate horizon, to which we travel
either in body or mind.

# 10TH HOUSE

### RULED BY CAPRICORN

Our aims and ambitions in life, what we aspire
to and what we're prepared to do to achieve it;
this is how we approach our working lives.

# 11TH HOUSE

### RULED BY AQUARIUS

The house of humanity and our
friendships, our relationships with the
wider world, our tribe or group to which
we feel an affiliation.

# 12TH HOUSE

### RULED BY PISCES

Our spiritual side resides here. Whether this
is religious or not, it embodies our inner life,
beliefs and the deeper connections we forge.

# THE FOUR ELEMENTS

The 12 astrological signs are divided into four groups, representing the four elements: fire, water, earth and air. This gives each of the three signs in each group additional characteristics.

# FIRE

ARIES ❧ LEO ❧ SAGITTARIUS

Embodying warmth, spontaneity and enthusiasm.

# WATER

CANCER ∿ SCORPIO ∿ PISCES

Embody a more feeling, spiritual and intuitive side.

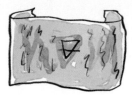

# EARTH

## TAURUS ❧ VIRGO ❧ CAPRICORN

Grounded and sure-footed and sometimes rather stubborn.

  ♈ ARIES

# AIR

GEMINI ☙ LIBRA ☙ AQUARIUS

Flourishing in the world of vision, ideas and perception.

# FIXED,
# CARDINAL OR
# MUTABLE?

The 12 signs are further divided into three groups of four, giving additional characteristics of being fixed, cardinal or mutable. These represent the way in which they respond to situations.

# FIXED

## TAURUS, LEO, SCORPIO AND AQUARIUS ARE FIXED SIGNS

Their energy tends to be steady and they are less reactive, more responsive, although they can have a tendency to be resistant to change and need encouragement.

# CARDINAL

## ARIES, CANCER, LIBRA AND CAPRICORN ARE CARDINAL SIGNS

Their energy is often instinctive and action-oriented, enabling them to get things started, although there's sometimes a tendency to fail to carry things through.

# MUTABLE

## GEMINI, VIRGO, SAGITTARIUS AND PISCES ARE MUTABLE SIGNS

The clue here is their adaptability and responsiveness to change, which they don't fear, and readiness to listen to and embrace new ideas.

# MERCURY RETROGRADE

This occurs several times over the astrological year and lasts for around four weeks, with a shadow week either side (a quick Google search will tell you the forthcoming dates). It's important what sign Mercury is in while it's retrograde, because its impact will be affected by the characteristics of that sign. For example, if Mercury is retrograde in Gemini, the sign of communication that is ruled by Mercury, the effect will be keenly felt in all areas of communication. However, if Mercury is retrograde in Aquarius, which rules the house of friendships and relationships, this may keenly affect our communication with large groups, or if in Sagittarius, which rules the house of travel, it could affect travel itineraries and encourage us to check our documents carefully.

Mercury retrograde can also be seen as an opportunity to pause, review or reconsider ideas and plans, to regroup, recalibrate and recuperate, and generally to take stock of where we are and how we might proceed. In our fast-paced 24/7 lives, Mercury retrograde can often be a useful opportunity to slow down and allow ourselves space to restore some necessary equilibrium.

# SATURN RETURN

When the planet Saturn returns to the place in your chart that it occupied at the time of your birth, it has an impact. This occurs roughly every 28 years, so we can see immediately that it correlates with ages that we consider representative of different life stages and when we might anticipate change or adjustment to a different era. At 28 we can be considered at full adult maturity, probably established in our careers and relationships, maybe with children; at 56 we have reached middle age and are possibly at another of life's crossroads; and at 84, we might be considered at the full height of our wisdom, our lives almost complete. If you know the time and place of your birth date, an online Saturn return calculator can give you the exact timing.

It will also be useful to identify in which astrological sign Saturn falls in your chart, which will help you reflect on its influence, as both influences can be very illuminating about how you will experience and manage the impact of its return. Often the time leading up to a personal Saturn return is a demanding one, but the lessons learnt help inform the decisions made about how to progress your own goals. Don't fear this period, but work with its influence: knowledge is power and Saturn has a powerful energy you can harness should you choose.

# THE MINOR PLANETS

S un sign astrology seldom makes mention of these 'minor'
planets that also orbit the sun, but increasingly their subtle
influence is being referenced. If you have had your birth chart
done (if you know your birth time and place you can do this online)
you will have access to this additional information.

Like the 10 main planets on the previous pages, these 18 minor
entities will also be positioned in an astrological sign, bringing their
energy to bear on these characteristics. You may, for example, have
Fortuna in Leo, or Diana in Sagittarius. Look to these for their subtle
influences on your birth chart and life via the sign they inhabit, all
of which will serve to animate and resonate further the information
you can reference on your own personal journey.

## AESCULAPIA

Jupiter's grandson and a powerful healer, Aesculapia was taught by Chiron and influences us in what could be life-saving action, realised through the characteristics of the sign in which it falls in our chart.

## BACCHUS

Jupiter's son, Bacchus is similarly benevolent but can sometimes lack restraint in the pursuit of pleasure. How this plays out in your chart is dependent on the sign in which it falls.

## APOLLO

Jupiter's son, gifted in art, music and healing, Apollo rides the Sun across the skies. His energy literally lights up the way in which you inspire others, characterised by the sign in which it falls in your chart.

## CERES

Goddess of agriculture and mother of Proserpina, Ceres is associated with the seasons and how we manage cycles of change in our lives. This energy is influenced by the sign in which it falls in our chart.

## CHIRON

Teacher of the gods, Chiron knew all about healing herbs and medical practices and he lends his energy to how we tackle the impossible or the unthinkable, that which seems difficult to do.

## DIANA

Jupiter's independent daughter was allowed to run free without the shackles of marriage. Where this falls in your birth chart will indicate what you are not prepared to sacrifice in order to conform.

## CUPID

Son of Venus. The sign into which Cupid falls will influence how you inspire love and desire in others, not always appropriately and sometimes illogically but it can still be an enduring passion.

## FORTUNA

Jupiter's daughter, who is always shown blindfolded, influences your fated role in other people's lives, how you show up for them without really understanding why, and at the right time.

## HYGEIA

Daughter of Aesculapia and also associated with health, Hygeia is about how you anticipate risk and the avoidance of unwanted outcomes. The way you do this is characterised by the sign in which Hygeia falls.

## MINERVA

Another of Jupiter's daughters, depicted by an owl, will show you via the energy given to a particular astrological sign in your chart how you show up at your most intelligent and smart. How you operate intellectually.

## JUNO

Juno was the wife of Jupiter and her position in your chart will indicate where you will make a commitment in order to feel safe and secure. It's where you might seek protection in order to flourish.

## OPS

The wife of Saturn, Ops saved the life of her son Jupiter by giving her husband a stone to eat instead of him. Her energy in our chart enables us to find positive solutions to life's demands and dilemmas.

PANACEA

Gifted with healing powers, Panacea provides us with a remedy for all ills and difficulties, and how this plays out in your life will depend on the characteristics of the astrological sign in which her energy falls.

PSYCHE

Psyche, Venus' daughter-in-law, shows us that part of ourselves that is easy to love and endures through adversity, and your soul that survives death and flies free, like the butterfly that depicts her.

PROSERPINA

Daughter of Ceres, abducted by Pluto, Proserpina has to spend her life divided between earth and the underworld and she represents how we bridge the gulf between different and difficult aspects of our lives.

SALACIA

Neptune's wife, Salacia stands on the seashore bridging land and sea, happily bridging the two realities. In your chart, she shows how you can harmoniously bring two sides of yourself together.

## VESTA

Daughter of Saturn, Vesta's job was to protect Rome and in turn she was protected by vestal virgins. Her energy influences how we manage our relationships with competitive females and male authority figures.

## VULCAN

Vulcan was a blacksmith who knew how to control fire and fashion metal into shape, and through the sign in which it falls in your chart will show you how you control your passion and make it work for you.

# FURTHER READING

*Jung's Studies in Astrology: Prophecies, Magic and the Qualities of Time*,

Liz Greene, Routledge (2018)

*Lunar Oracle: Harness the Power of the Moon*,

Liberty Phi, OH Editions (2021)

*Metaphysics of Astrology: Why Astrology Works*,

Ivan Antic, Independently published (2020)

*Parkers' Astrology: The Definitive Guide to Using Astrology in Every Aspect of Your Life*,

Julia and Derek Parker, Dorling Kindersley (2020)

## USEFUL WEBSITES

Alicebellastrology.com
Astro.com
Astrology.com
Cafeastrology.com
Costarastrology.com
Jessicaadams.com

## USEFUL APPS

Astro Future
Co-Star
Moon
Sanctuary
Time Nomad
Time Passages

## ACKNOWLEDGEMENTS

Thanks are due to my Taurean publisher Kate Pollard for commissioning this Astrology Oracle series, to Piscean Matt Tomlinson for his careful editing, and to Evi O Studio for their beautiful design and illustrations.

## ABOUT THE AUTHOR

As a sun sign Aquarius Liberty Phi loves to explore the world and has lived on three different continents, currently residing in North America. Their Gemini moon inspires them to communicate their love of astrology and other esoteric practices while Leo rising helps energise them. Their first publication, also released by OH Editions, is a box set of 36 oracle cards and accompanying guide, entitled *Lunar Oracle: Harness the Power of the Moon*.

*Published in 2023 by OH Editions,
an imprint of Welbeck Non-Fiction Ltd,
part of the Welbeck Publishing Group.
Offices in London, 20 Mortimer Street, London, W1T 3JW,
and Sydney, 205 Commonwealth Street, Surry Hills, 2010.
www.welbeckpublishing.com*

*Design © 2023 OH Editions
Text © 2023 Liberty Phi
Illustrations © 2023 Evi O. Studio*

*A CIP catalogue record for this book is available from the British Library.*

*ISBN 978-1-91431-793-4*

*Publisher: Kate Pollard
Editor: Sophie Elletson
In-house editor: Matt Tomlinson
Designer: Evi O. Studio
Illustrator: Evi O. Studio
Production controller: Jess Brisley
Printed and bound by Leo Paper*

MIX
Paper | Supporting
responsible forestry
FSC® C020056

*10 9 8 7 6 5 4 3 2 1*